Abyssinian Cats

Wendy Perkins
AR B.L.: 1.5
Points: 0.5

LG

Pebble®

Abyssinian Cats

by Wendy Perkins

Consulting Editor: Gail Saunders-Smith, PhD

Consultant: Jennifer Zablotny, DVM
Member, American Veterinary Medical Association

Capstone press®
Mankato, Minnesota

Pebble Books are published by Capstone Press,
151 Good Counsel Drive, P.O. Box 669, Mankato, Minnesota 56002.
www.capstonepress.com

Printed in the United States of America

1 2 3 4 5 6 13 12 11 10 09 08

Library of Congress Cataloging-in-Publication Data
Perkins, Wendy, 1957–
Abyssinian cats / by Wendy Perkins.
p. cm. — (Pebble Books. Cats)
Includes bibliographical references and index.
ISBN-13: 978-1-4296-1214-2 (hardcover)
ISBN-10: 1-4296-1214-2 (hardcover)
1. Abyssinian cat — Juvenile literature. I. Title. II. Series.
SF449.A28P47 2008
636.8′26 — dc22 2007017790

Summary: Simple text and photographs present an introduction to the Abyssinian cat breed, its growth from kitten to adult, and pet care information.

Note to Parents and Teachers

The Cats set supports national science standards related to life science. This book describes and illustrates Abyssinian cats. The images support early readers in understanding the text. The repetition of words and phrases helps early readers learn new words. This book also introduces early readers to subject-specific vocabulary words, which are defined in the Glossary section. Early readers may need assistance to read some words and to use the Table of Contents, Glossary, Read More, Internet Sites, and Index sections of the book.

Table of Contents

Friendly Cats

Abyssinian cats are playful and friendly. Most people call them Abys.

Say it like this:
Abyssinian
(ab-uh-SIH-nee-uhn)

Abys have short,
smooth coats.
Each hair has dark
and light bands,
called ticking.

Abys have
triangle-shaped heads.
They also have
large eyes and ears.

From Kitten to Adult

Aby kittens have blue eyes. Their eyes turn green or gold as they grow up.

Very young kittens
fit in your hand.
They grow quickly.

Adult Abys weigh about
10 pounds (4 kilograms).
They are quieter
than most cats.
Abys meow softly.

Caring for Abys

Abys rarely need
to be brushed.
Their rough tongues
clean off dirt and
loose hair.

Abys are active cats.
They need places
where they can run
and climb.

Abys like to stay
close to their owners.
Abys make good pets.

Glossary

active — being able to exercise, play, and move around

coat — a cat's fur

friendly — kind

meow — the noise a cat makes

owner — a person who has something; pets need owners who care for them.

rarely — not often

rough — not smooth; a cat's rough tongue has bumps.

ticking — bands of light and dark color on a hair

Read More

Ganeri, Anita. *Cats.* Heinemann First Library. A Pet's Life. Chicago: Heinemann, 2003.

Shores, Erika L. *Caring for Your Cat.* First Facts. Positively Pets. Mankato, Minn.: Capstone Press, 2007.

Internet Sites

FactHound offers a safe, fun way to find Internet sites related to this book. All of the sites on FactHound have been researched by our staff.

Here's how:

1. Visit *www.facthound.com*
2. Choose your grade level.
3. Type in this book **ID 1429612142** for age-appropriate sites. You may also browse subjects by clicking on letters, or by clicking on pictures and words.
4. Click on the **Fetch It** button.

FactHound will fetch the best sites for you!

Index

Word Count: 119
Grade: 1
Early-Intervention Level: 16

Editorial Credits
Erika L. Shores, editor; Renée T. Doyle, set designer; Veronica Bianchini, and Ted Williams, contributing designers; Linda Clavel, photo researcher

Photo Credits
Nature Picture Library/Jane Burton, 12
Norvia Behling, 14, 20
Photo Researchers Inc./M. E. Browning, 16
Ron Kimball Stock/Alan Robinson, 4
Shutterstock/MAGDALENA SZACHOWSKA, cover, 1, 8, 22
Vivace Cattery/Rita Bruche, 6, 10, 18